THE POWER OF A Promise

GARY KEESEE

ISBN: 978-1-958486-77-1

Published by Free Indeed Publishers.

Distributed by Faith Life Now.

Faith Life Now
P.O. Box 779
New Albany, OH 43054
1-(888)-391-LIFE

You can reach Faith Life Now on the Internet at www.faithlifenow.com.

DEDICATION

*Dedicated to my ministry partners,
who are helping to send the Kingdom around
the world.
And to my life partner, wife, and encourager,
Drenda.*

CONTENTS

HOW MANY YEARS DO YOU WANT TO WAIT?

Chapter 1

Many years ago, my wife, Drenda, and I lived hand-to-mouth. We lived in downright poverty. Sure, we were believers, and we had a great family life. We enjoyed our marriage and our family, but we were struggling, *really* struggling.

We went to a church that taught us how God loves us and that He has great things planned for our lives, but we weren't living it. **We weren't experiencing God's promises in our lives.** We were barely surviving.

Pawnshops were a way of life. Everything we had was used, *very* used. The carpet on our kids' bedroom floors had been retrieved from a trash bin. Their mattresses came from a nursing home. We had two cars, but—with more than 200,000 miles on each of them—they had definitely seen better days. The floorboards in both of them were rusting out, and they were beat up and bent up.

The little, 1800s farmhouse our family of seven lived in had also seen better days. Not only did we have weeds growing through the broken windows, it seemed we were living in a house that already belonged to families of spiders and bees!

The big, black spiders we lived with were really bold. They'd come running across the floor at us or up over our beds while we were in them. And the bees—there were so many wasps and yellow jackets coming in that house that we would have to pull our sheets down on our beds at night and check for them! Many times, when we were getting dressed for church, we would hear a scream because somebody would put their arm in a sleeve or a jacket, and there'd be bees in there! Our kids got stung all of the time! But the spiders and bees weren't half of our problems.

For years, our finances had been on a slippery downhill slope. Working on straight commissions in the insurance industry had left us with too much month at the end of our money time and time again. And while I always intended to pay off our debts, or whatever we may have borrowed each month, we only ended up further behind.

For nine *very long* years, we were in financial chaos. Not only did we owe on our broken-down farmhouse and two rusted-out, bent up, high mileage cars, we also had ten maxed out credit cards, three finance company loans at interest rates of 28%, more than $13,000 owed in back taxes, more than $26,000 owed to relatives, and judgments and liens filed against us!

To say we lived under intense financial pressure would be an understatement!

I remember one specific time I had to mail an envelope. We had borrowed money from anybody and everybody we could. We had exhausted all of our options. In fact, we owed money to nearly anyone you could imagine—hospitals, dry cleaners—everyone. So I had a letter I needed to mail, but *I couldn't even afford the stamp.*

I called my dad to ask if he had change I could have to buy a stamp.

He said, "Do I have to breathe for you, too?"

My dad was funding everything, and he wasn't a believer at the time. Drenda and I were the believers! But for nine years we lived like that.

I was sick during those days, too. I was miserable. I lived in stress. I was anxious and fearful. The doctors put me on medication to deal with the panic attacks I was having, but that only seemed to make things worse. Fear consumed my life. I even got to the point of not wanting to leave my house. You can imagine what that did to my sales business!

Everyday life became a game of survival, and I was

constantly looking over my shoulder, waiting for the next thing to go wrong or blow up. I had no joy and no peace. The stress I lived under didn't make me a great husband or father either. The word my family heard most of the time was, "NO." I was constantly telling them, "No, you can't have that," or "No, we can't do that."

I reached the end of my rope when an attorney called our house one morning and warned me that his firm was going to file a lawsuit against me if I didn't give them $1,900 within three days.

Needless to say, I was desperate. I had exhausted all of my options. I knew it was over; I had nowhere to turn.

I clearly remember collapsing on my bed, desperately crying out to God. To be honest, I was shocked that God spoke to me immediately. He told me that I had trusted in debt to meet my needs and that I had never taken the time to learn how His Kingdom operated. He then went on and told me that most of His body, the Church, was in debt and that He wanted them free financially. He said, "Take the time to learn how my Kingdom operates."

Our lives completely changed after that. Drenda and I began to learn how the Kingdom operated, and what we learned was amazing. When we discovered and began to apply Kingdom principles, it was like a light switch came on, and we truly began experiencing the promises of God in our lives. In less than three years from that day, we were completely out of debt. We started new businesses during that time that kept growing. We paid cash for our cars, cash for our 55 acres of land, and built and paid for our new home. We were extremely excited, and still are! In fact, we've been on a mission ever since to help others experience the Kingdom of God.

We lived that broken life for nine very long years.

We had waited nine *very long* years to have what the Bible says is ours. The sad thing is <u>we didn't have to wait those nine years.</u> **The Kingdom was always available to us.**

How many years do YOU want to wait?

In Luke 13, we read the story of a woman who waited 18 years:

> *On a Sabbath Jesus was teaching in one of the synagogues, and a woman was there who had been crippled by a spirit for eighteen years. She*

was bent over and could not straighten up at all. When Jesus saw her, he called her forward and said to her, "Woman, you are set free from your infirmity." Then he put his hands on her, and immediately she straightened up and praised God.

Indignant because Jesus had healed on the Sabbath, the synagogue leader said to the people, "There are six days for work. So come and be healed on those days, not on the Sabbath."

The Lord answered him, "You hypocrites! Doesn't each of you on the Sabbath untie your ox or donkey from the stall and lead it out to give it water? Then should not this woman, a daughter of Abraham, whom Satan has kept bound for eighteen long years, be set free on the Sabbath day from what bound her?"

When he said this, all his opponents were humiliated, but the people were delighted with all the wonderful things he was doing.

This Scripture tells us something very important. Jesus says, "Should not this woman be set free?" He then goes into a legal dialogue, explaining why she should be free. He says she doesn't need to suffer any longer in bondage by Satan. Jesus refers to her suffering as, "these eighteen long years." That's a very long time to be in bondage. Nine years was too long. Eighteen years is a nightmare.

Why did the woman suffer for eighteen years? Religion has no answers. Religion is more concerned with its protocol and formulas than it is with people. We see it plainly in this Scripture—the synagogue leader was indignant. Jesus wasn't following his rules.

But Jesus reminded him that *the woman had a legal right to healing.* As a daughter of Abraham, *she had legal rights.* She had *the promise* of freedom. She had *the promise* of healing. She had the legality of the Kingdom of God backing her healing. So, why shouldn't she be healed? Why should she have to live another day in bondage?

Are you living your life the same way as this woman— and Drenda and I—lived? **What are you waiting for?**

Why can't you have what the Bible says is yours? Why do you have to wait any longer? Just like the woman Jesus freed, the Bible says you are a child of God.

> *Yet to all who did receive him, to those who believed in his name, he gave the right to become children of God.*
> – John 1:12

As a child of God, you don't have to endure years of hardship. You have legal rights. You don't have to go through years of chaos and mess. You don't have to live a broken life.

You don't have to just survive life. You don't have to live with the stress and the anxiety. You don't have to live life just waiting for Friday, so you can stop the rat race. I know how exhausting that is! There's no pleasure in it.

When Drenda and I discovered the Kingdom of God, our lives completely changed. We were able to truly enjoy life. It was fun.

You should be having fun, too. You should see the results of your labor. You should be doing much more than just enduring.

It's time you truly experience God's promises in your life.

Don't wait any longer.

THE ANSWER

Chapter 2

Drenda and I went from the broken-down, 1800s farmhouse to a house that we designed ourselves. It has six bedrooms, four bathrooms, crown molding, hardwood floors, and new appliances. I specifically mention crown molding and new appliances because sometimes it's the small things that make a big difference. New appliances may seem like a small thing to some, but for so many years we would get our appliances used. We had the classic avocado green refrigerator and stove many years after they were out of style—in fact, they were both more than 20 years old.

Our home also sits on 55 beautiful acres with about 20 acres of woods and 15 acres of marshland. If you know anything about me, I love hunting, and this land provides some of the best hunting for deer and ducks in the entire state of Ohio.

It was really a dream come true. We took all of our kids to the closing and boy, did we celebrate when we walked out of that meeting. We had gone from barely being able to pay $300 a month to rent our farmhouse to paying cash for our land, building our dream home with more than 7,000 square feet of space, and having it debt free. That was quite a ride!

Now, I don't share any of this to brag. I just want you to imagine how it felt. As I said in the last chapter, we were so excited!

We were constantly pinching ourselves to make sure it was really happening! We'd drive down the road in our new car saying, "Can you believe this is a new car? It smells like a new car! This is a new car!" When we watched the basement being dug for our new house, we stood and cried. We just couldn't believe that was our house. When we got in the house, we lay awake at night and still couldn't believe it.

And I had peace.

When we got out of debt, I had peace. Sure, it was good to have some nice things, and it was nice to have a beautiful house to go home to. But having peace trumped any "thing" in my life—the peace that came from knowing something wasn't going to break. The peace that came from knowing that my wife could get in a car and have it start, and that she could drive our five kids around and not be at risk of having the car break down.

And I found my purpose.

Before we were financially free, my life was consumed with finding money. Nearly every thought of every day was about how we would survive, how I would find the money we needed to pay our bills, how I could find the sales. I was consumed with money and surviving.

But when we got out of debt and had money in the bank, our cars paid for, our house paid for, my focus changed. I didn't have to worry about how I'd buy groceries for my family. I didn't have to worry about how I would pay to fix the car. I could think about other things. I could discover why I'm on the earth to begin with.

How did all of this happen for Drenda and me? What had changed?

There's a lot to the story but—to make a long story short—**we discovered real answers on how to release the Kingdom of God into our lives.**

See, so many people are waiting for God to do something for them, but what they don't realize is that Jesus already paid for it all! There is a way to live that is completely different than the survival mentality that we all grew up with. That's the purpose of this book: to help you learn what

Drenda and I learned. And, even though there are many principles and things we learned, there is one principle that I believe is an *absolute*—a game changer. It's so important that I've written this entire book about it—the power of a promise.

YOU HAVE TO LEARN THIS PRINCIPLE.

There are many aspects of the Kingdom that you need to learn in order to effectively walk out your God-designed future, but learning the power of a promise is especially important. In fact, I believe you'll never experience what the Kingdom can do until you learn this principle.

This powerful principle is found in a small, but profound, section of Scripture that reveals Kingdom law:

> *His divine power has given us everything we need for life and godliness through our knowledge of him who called us by his own glory and goodness. Through these he has given us his very great and precious promises so that through them you may participate in the divine nature and escape the corruption in the world caused by evil desires.*
> — 2 Peter 1:3–4 *(NIV, 1984)*

Notice this Scripture doesn't say, "His divine power has given us a *few* things," or "His divine power has given us only *enough* to just barely make it through life and to get to heaven." That's because we're not supposed to just hang on! We're not supposed to just suffer a few more weary days and then go to heaven. Sure, going to heaven is the most important thing, and I praise God for that.

But God doesn't take us home to heaven when we're born again. We became citizens of heaven the moment we were born again, but we still live here on the earth, and we have to know how to operate effectively on the earth. But living on the earth doesn't negate our citizenship in heaven or our legal rights as citizens of heaven.

We're on assignment here, and while we're here we need to know how to tap into our legal rights as citizens of heaven and enjoy some heaven on earth. After all, people are attracted to life done right, not religion. People want to see heaven on the earth. Heaven is the answer everyone needs.

Drenda and I were active and devoted church members. We loved going to church, but we were going bankrupt. Our broken-down, impoverished way of life wasn't winning many converts. But we found an answer in 2 Peter 1:3: *"His divine power has given us EVERYTHING...."*

Now, some people have trouble with the word "everything." That's because they don't believe it. They may go to church and hear the Word, but they can't say out of their mouths, with confidence, that God has given them "everything" because they don't see it in their own lives. In fact, their lives may flat out seem to contradict what this Scripture says.

We've all grown up in this corrupt, earth-curse system. Lack, fear, and worry are all we know in this system. We've lived in survival mode for so long that we've trained ourselves to think in terms of disappointment, hardships, and sickness. **But there's no shortage in the Kingdom of heaven.**

So, when Peter says God has given us everything we need for life and godliness, <u>that's your answer for life and for absolutely any problem you face.</u>

The Word of God tells us that God's divine power has given us everything we need for life *and* godliness. I think we can understand what Peter meant when he said everything we need for *life,* but he didn't stop there. He added, "*and godliness.*" What is "godliness"? Well, you could also say "righteousness" or God's definition of how our lives should be lived from His perspective of our created purpose.

How does God want us to live life? What is His perspective? Look at Adam—the first man. Did Adam worry about lack of provision or sickness? Absolutely not. Scripture shows us that man was created at the end of the sixth day *after* everything had already been created on the earth that he would need for life. *Everything* that man needed had been created for him. Everything. There was no lack and no sickness. So, a life lived in the Kingdom is a life lived as God always intended, with full provision and no fear.

Of course, God's right way of living is in stark contrast to how life as we know it in the earth-curse system functions. The earth-curse system refers to the curse that came on the earth after Adam rebelled against God and Satan became the "god of this world ," as Paul says in 2 Corinthians 4:4. Sickness, disease, death, and poverty came upon the earth at that time. Life became hard and fear became a way of life. But now, through Jesus Christ, we find an escape from the fear and destruction all around us and have abundant life (John 10:10, KJV).

NO MATTER WHAT YOU'VE HEARD, GOD IS GOOD

Chapter 3

So, how do we tap into the provision and have everything God has given us for life? Look at 2 Peter 1:3 again,

> *His divine power has given us everything we need for life and godliness* **through** *our knowledge of him who called us by his own glory and goodness.*

Peter is saying we have to have knowledge to be able to walk above the earth-curse system of defeat. Not just any knowledge, but knowledge of HIM—of *God*—who Peter then says called us "by his own glory and *goodness.*"

Read that again.

Because people miss this absolutely critical piece all the time:

God is good.

See, the devil has convinced most people that God is against them. Satan doesn't want you to know that God is good. He wants to slant God's character so that you won't trust Him and you won't serve Him. But James tells us not to be deceived:

> *Don't be deceived, my dear brothers and sisters. Every good and perfect gift is from above, coming*

*down from the Father of the heavenly lights, who
does not change like shifting shadows.*
— James 1:16-17

People think horrible things about God. You hear it everywhere you go: "God allows bad things to happen to good people." Christians cry out, "I don't know why God isn't helping me! I work for Him all the time, and I'm a good person. Why isn't He helping me?"

People think God does things to teach them lessons, that He's mad at them, that He "takes" children, that He causes tornadoes ... that He gives people cancer. If you thought this way about God, you'd never believe a promise He made to you about supplying everything you need. No way! You'd run from Him as fast as you could!

So many people don't believe that God is good. In fact, most people believe that God sends people to hell. But the Bible tells us that hell wasn't created for man; hell was created for Satan and his angels (Matthew 25:41). The judgment of hell was Satan's judgment, not mankind's judgment. It was only when Adam joined Satan's rebellion against God that he fell under the same judgment as Satan.

That's where so many people get it wrong. They

think that they'll stand before God and He'll decide whether they're going to heaven or hell—based on wrong reasons like their works or if they were a good person or not. But God is going to look at only one thing when it comes to our judgment. If we've made Jesus our Lord and Savior, our names are written in the Lamb's Book of Life, and we can escape Satan's judgment (Revelation 21:27).

Because it doesn't matter how many good things you do or how often you pray. Most Christians don't even realize that every person born in the earth realm is already headed to hell because of what *Adam* did, NOT because of what they've done. That's why God sent Jesus. Jesus is our escape from Satan's dominion. Jesus is our escape from receiving the same judgment as Satan and his angels. Jesus is our escape from the earth-curse system, our escape to the Kingdom of heaven.

But let's back up a bit.

Peter is saying that **without a proper understanding of who God is—that He is good and His desire toward us is also good—we can never receive His answer for us.** Because how can you believe God and trust what He says if you don't believe He is good?

So, if you believe that God is against you, that He harms mankind, or that He enjoys withholding good things from you, you'll never enjoy the "everything" we're talking about here. This is because your understanding of the word "everything" can't be complete if you don't know God.

No matter how many bad things you've heard about God, they're not true. God is good, and He's good *all* of the time. If you're having trouble believing that, the Bible instructs you to reflect on creation for a moment:

> *For since the creation of the world God's invisible qualities—his eternal power and divine nature— have been clearly seen, being understood from what has been made, so that people are without excuse.*
>
> — Romans 1:20

God's goodness is clearly evident in creation. Every flower, every sunrise and sunset, and every star in the sky point to God's amazing power and goodness, all declaring to you how much He loves you. Before you can accept the idea that God has already given you everything you need for life, you must get your image of God corrected.

*His divine power has given us everything we need for life and godliness through our knowledge of him who called **us by his own glory and goodness**.*

— *Peter 1:3*

You can see that God's goodness is only one part of Him. While His goodness is His will—His intent—toward us, Peter also talks about His *glory*. God's glory is the vastness of who He is, His immeasurable power and dominion. His glory has the means to back up what He has said.

So, we can enjoy God's promise that He would give us everything we need for life and godliness because His glory and goodness make His promise to us valid. His glory—the majesty of His estate—which is immeasurable, and His goodness (which He expresses to us through His promise to us) guarantee us what He has promised.

Second Peter 1:3-4 were the answer Drenda and I had been looking for. For years, we had no evidence in our lives that God's will was for us to have everything we needed. In fact, we thought God was holding out on us. We thought that, for whatever reason, He just wasn't bringing the financial answers we needed. But based on this Scripture, the truth was that <u>we needed knowledge of who God is</u>. We couldn't receive from Him or fully believe His promises to us because we had a faulty picture of Him!

That's when we started really taking the time to look in the Word of God to discover who God really is, and that He is good all the time. It was only then that we became convinced that it was His will that we have everything we need in life.

Peter says that there are three things you need to know if you are going to receive from God:

1. **<u>GOD IS GOOD.</u>**

2. **<u>GOD HAS THE MEANS TO BACK UP WHAT HE SAYS.</u>**

3. **<u>IT IS HIS WILL TO GIVE US EVERYTHING WE NEED FOR LIFE.</u>**

With these three things established, Peter goes on in 2 Peter 1:3-4 to say that God has given us promises (that are good and that He can back up) and that— through these promises—we may participate with the divine nature and escape!

> *Through these (his glory and goodness) he has given us his very great and precious promises so that through them you may participate in the divine nature and escape the corruption in the world caused by evil desires.*

Notice it says that through God's very great and *precious promises* we can participate in the divine nature. To give you an idea of what that means, let's assume that I told you I was going to give you $5 billion. If you knew I had the means to do so, and I wasn't kidding, you'd have to agree that my promise was "great" and extremely precious to you. That gives you an idea of how great God's promises are! They're mind-boggling! Except God's promises are worth so much more than $5 billion!

You can get an idea of how precious the promises of God are, but what does it mean to "participate in the divine nature"? After all, Peter says that participating in the divine nature is a prerequisite for being able to escape the earth-curse system that we live in.

First, let's define our terms. When Peter refers to God's "divine nature," he's referring to how God does things, or how He acts. This is the same as children behaving like their parents. They eat with spoons and forks; they walk on two feet, sleep, hunger, etc., all just like their parents do because they're made in the image of their parents. They act with the same nature their parents do, or just like them.

So, when Peter tells us that we can participate with the divine nature, he is telling us that there is a specific way that God does things that will allow us to escape the corruption in the world system.

GOD SPEAKS IN THE PAST TENSE: YOU ALREADY HAVE EVERYTHING HE'S PROMISED

Chapter 4

But what's the connection? How does a promise allow us to participate in the divine nature of God? To find out, let's go to Romans 4:16-17:

> *Therefore, the promise comes by faith, so that it may be by grace and may be guaranteed to all Abraham's offspring—not only to those who are of the law but also to those who have the faith of Abraham. He is the father of us all. As it is written: "I have made you a father of many nations." He is our father in the sight of God, in whom he believed—the God who gives life to the dead and calls into being things that were not.*

See where God told Abraham that He had made him a father of many nations? That's a reference to Genesis 17:5. Do you remember how many children Abraham had when God said that to him? NONE! In fact, Abraham even laughed about it when God said it to him because he was so old. Here's the thing: If Abraham didn't have any children when God said that to him, why did God say it in the *past* tense? Why did God say, "I *have made* you a father of many nations" instead of "I *will* make you a father of many nations"?

Because two chapters earlier—in Genesis 15—God had already **promised** Abraham an heir. In fact, God had promised him millions and millions of heirs!

> *Then the word of the Lord came to him: "This man will not be your heir, but a son who is your own flesh and*

blood will be your heir." He took him outside and said, "Look up at the sky and count the stars—if indeed you can count them." Then he said to him, "So shall your offspring be."

— Genesis 15:4-5

Romans 4:17b gives us a glimpse into the divine nature, or how God operates, and explains how God could say Abraham already had children when he had none: *"God who gives life to the dead and calls into being things that were not."*

I'm sure you would agree that God has the power to call something into existence that wasn't there and that He has the power to give life to the dead. So, when God gave Abraham that promise, He was calling something that was not as though it were, because He has the power (glory) to do just that. He made His will (His goodness) known to Abraham through a promise. And since God can't lie, once He spoke His intentions, it was finished.

This is an important key: A PROMISE CALLS SOMETHING THAT IS NOT AS THOUGH IT IS!

Imagine for a moment that I give you a check for $1,000. You are excited the moment I hand it to you, right? Because in your mind you have $1,000, and you imagine how you can spend it. In fact, if I ask you how much money you have at the moment, you will say $1,000. But the fact is you don't have $1,000; you have a promise of $1,000.

A check is called a promissory note because it's simply a promise. It's only made good (when you cash it) by the one who signed it. Since you know I have more than enough money to back up the $1,000 (the "glory" of who I am, my estate) and I actually gave it to you (my goodness expressed to you), you count it as done. THE PROMISE (the check) IS AS GOOD AS THE MONEY. You act on the promise as if you had the money.

You really need to go back and read that again.

You consider the check as "good" because you know of my estate and my intention toward you, so you act just like you have the actual cash in your hand. This is exactly what Peter is saying. Based on God's glory and goodness (His ability to back up His word), He has given us very great and precious promises. He signed the checks so that through them—the promises, the "signed checks"— we could participate in the divine nature (calling things that are not as those they were) and <u>escape.</u>

So we see that a promise calls something that is not as though it were. When we receive a promise as valid, we act like we already have it! Just like you act as if you already have the money from a signed check you believe is "good," when you believe the Word of God and His promises, you can participate with God, or do what He does, by acting as if His Word was true (past tense) and is already yours.

As we agree with God, we begin to act like God does,

calling things that are not as those they were. We are participating in the divine nature, or acting just like God does.

One important thing I need to point out here, though, is that the promises *allow* us to participate in the divine nature. It's our choice, and it's optional. But participating in the divine nature is our only escape. So, if you want to live outside of the box and live a life driven from God's perspective of having all things, then you need to know that <u>to participate infers that you are actively doing something.</u> In this case, you can participate with God.

Let's say you are sick and you find a promise from God that says,

> *Is anyone among you sick? Let them call the elders of the church to pray over them and anoint them with oil in the name of the Lord. And the prayer offered in faith will make the sick person well; the Lord will raise them up. If they have sinned, they will be forgiven.*
> — *James 5:14-15*

This Scripture is very clear. If anyone is sick, it tells you what you should do. The promise is that you will be healed and raised up. If you believe God's promise and did what God said to do, then how would you act? You would say, "I've *been* healed." You wouldn't say, "I'm trying to *get* healed" or "I'm believing God to heal me." No, God gave you His very great promise so that you can participate in His divine nature (act like He does) calling things that are not as though they were. Your claim to speak like you have something when it looks like you don't is valid because you have a check (the promise) in your pocket, made out to you, and signed by God himself!

But most people don't know this. They act and speak *in the future tense* concerning the promises of God, always claiming to be *waiting* for God to do what He said He *already* did. But that's not participating with the divine nature, calling things that aren't as those they were! That's participating in human nature, which is limited to what we can feel, see, and hear.

Let me give you an example from my own life. Years ago, I began to have some serious issues in my body. I had numbness in my arms and legs, heart palpitations, and I was having panic attacks. The doctors couldn't find anything wrong with me, but they put me on various medications to alleviate my symptoms. I didn't know what was going on with my body.

I became very sensitive to the food I ate. If I ate any kind of sugar, I would get very lethargic and incoherent, often almost passing out. Because of this, I was afraid to eat, and I avoided anything with sugar in it like it was a deadly poison. Sure, I knew that God healed, and I cried out to him for healing, but nothing changed.

When I heard that a minister who was known for praying

for the sick would be holding a meeting in a nearby town, my wife and I made plans to attend. During the service, I had great anticipation that I would be healed. When the minister laid his hands on me, the anointing of God was so strong that I literally fell to the ground. The power of God was so strong that I couldn't get up! My wife, Drenda, came over to me and laid her hand on me. The power of God that was on me was so strong that she also fell to the ground. We both lay there for about 20 minutes before making our way back to our seats.

As the meeting ended, the presence of God was still all over me, but I was puzzled because I still felt sick. I was confused. How could I not be healed with such an anointing of God's power on my body?

As we got ready for bed that night, I could still sense God's presence but nothing seemed to have changed in my body. During the night I had a dream. There were no people in my dream, but I heard words being spoken aloud by someone. I heard, "Therefore when you pray believe that you receive and you shall have it."

When I woke up, I told Drenda what I had just dreamt and asked her what she thought it meant. She very quickly said, "Gary, that is a Scripture. It's Mark 11:24." I remembered I had heard those words before, but what did it mean? I slowly reviewed the Scripture again and again until I finally got it:

When we pray we are to believe that we receive before we see it. We don't need to see it if we have God's promise.

I told Drenda, "I see it! I've been waiting for God to heal me, but all along, I've already been healed!"

Then, I was determined to prove it.

There's a root beer stand that Drenda and I always loved to go to before I was sick. Drenda knew what I knew—my body had an immediate reaction to sugar, and I avoided it at all costs. But after I received this revelation, I told Drenda, "Let's go get some root beer. I am healed."

We walked into the root beer store and up to the counter. They had frosted mugs in two sizes. I asked for the largest. As I was about to take my first sip, Drenda looked at me and said, "I agree! You are healed!" I drank the entire mug. It was the best tasting root beer I've ever had. It was so good that I ordered a second large mug. And, you know what? Nothing happened! There was no effect on my body. I've been healed ever since.

See, I had been making the mistake that so many people make: I thought I was waiting for the evidence to show up to validate my healing. But according to Scripture, I needed to operate in the divine nature based on God's promises to me. I needed to operate as God operates—like it was *already* done in order to escape the corruption in my body. And, praise God, it worked just like God said it would!

God has already helped you, too. He has already made a way of escape for you. He did all He could do for you when Jesus was nailed to the tree. Your legal right to complete freedom was insured at that moment. But you have to know God's character, or there's no hope. Once you understand and are convinced of His goodness and His glory and you *participate* in the divine nature, it will work for you, too.

I LIKE BUFFETS; HOW ABOUT YOU?

Chapter 5

So far, we've learned that by God's glory and His goodness He has given us His precious promises so that, through them, we can participate in the divine nature and escape. What are we escaping? Let's have a look:

> *His divine power has given us everything we need for life and godliness through our knowledge of him who called us by his own glory and goodness. Through these he has given us his very great and precious promises so that through them you may participate in the divine nature and escape the corruption in the world caused by evil desires.*
> — *2 Peter 1:3-4 (NIV, 1984)*

Peter makes it very clear that we are escaping the corruption in the world caused by evil desires or, as the King James Version says, "lust."

Desires and appetites for things are normal, but normal desires become evil when we try to fulfill them in an illegal manner. Why would someone stoop to doing something illegal to satisfy a normal desire? Because the desire isn't being satisfied. The King James uses the word *lust* instead of evil desires. People don't lust after something they already have; they lust after things they want but don't have.

God created man at the end of the sixth day. Why

the sixth day and not earlier? Because everything was complete and ready for man. There was no lack. Everything that man needed was already created for him on the earth. But Adam lost the provision of God when he rebelled. God then tells him in Genesis 3:17 that, because of him (Adam), the earth has become cursed and now he will have to survive by his own painful toil and sweat.

Since that day, mankind has been in survival mode, running after provision, and making decisions around money. You've probably heard this race to find money called the Rat Race. But Peter tells us there is an escape from this earth-curse system of lack and survival thinking.

What is the escape Peter talks about? It's that, through Jesus, we have access to a new Kingdom—the Kingdom of God—that has restored back to us an avenue to prosper in the earth realm.

So, your escape from the corrupted earth realm and its lack is that *God has already given you everything you need* (2 Peter 1:3). You don't need to be tempted to lust after things because *you already have everything* you need. The evil desires—the corruption of the earth—no longer apply to you if you apply the principle that Peter is teaching.

To teach this, I like to use the illustration of a buffet restaurant. Yes, as in food. Because anyone who knows me knows that I love buffets—especially Chinese food buffets. A lot of people like buffets because you can show up, get exactly what you want, eat as much as you want, and leave satisfied.

Most buffet restaurants are "all you can eat." So, say you've had your fill of the buffet and, on your way out the door, you pass the food line again. Do you think you would lust after that food? Do you think you'd envy the guy in line who has two plates loaded with food and think to yourself, "I wish I had two more plates like him?" Would you be jealous of what he had? Of course not! Because you're stuffed and already had all you cared to have.

Of course, if you're still hungry, you can go back and get some more. In fact, you can eat all you want! You have no reason to be envious or jealous of the other buffet-goers because you can go back any time you want, and you can have as much as you want.

Now, it may seem elementary, and you may not even like buffets, but I want you to really get this—**God has given you everything you need.**

Philippians 4:19 says,

And my God will meet all your needs according to the riches of his glory in Christ Jesus.

Just like being completely satisfied at the buffet restaurant, through the promises of God, you can participate in the divine nature and be completely satisfied every time. You don't have to lust after things. You don't have to be jealous and upset when you see someone with more than what you think they should have.

Psalm 23:5 says that *God has prepared a feast for you* even in the presence of your enemies.

This is the escape Peter is talking about—having everything that you need, having all that you want, and being satisfied. Because if you have everything you need, you won't be corrupted by evil desires. You won't be tempted to pursue wrong desires. You'll be satisfied.

Several years ago, I had preached at a conference in California and was taking a red-eye flight back to Ohio. I knew the weekend would be busy with three services to preach when I got home, and I was already tired. As I was heading to the airport, I was talking to my wife, Drenda, on the phone and she said, "Let's agree that you can fly home first class." I agreed and we prayed. Now, I very rarely fly first class, but sometimes if I really know I need rest, I will upgrade my seat. But when I got to the airport, it was clear that an upgrade wasn't happening. All of the first class seats were taken, and there was a list of 20 people ahead of me that were waiting for one, too.

As I sat down on the plane, there was a small commotion in front of me as a man voiced his complaint about not being able to sit with his wife. No one wanted to switch seats. After a few moments, I offered to give up my aisle seat and take a middle seat so they could sit together. The flight attendant was very thankful that I had helped make the couple comfortable. Little did I know how thankful.

About 30 minutes into the flight, the flight attendants started to serve the economy seats their normal drink and peanuts. The first class curtain had been drawn, but you could smell a full meal being served to the first class guests. Suddenly, the same flight attendant was in front of me in the aisle with a full first class tray in her hands. She had walked all the way back to me in row 27 and said, "I thought you might be hungry." It was great, because I was hungry!

And that wasn't all! She made trip after trip back to my row to bring me refreshments and refills throughout the entire flight. About an hour after the meal, she appeared with a full snack tray. This was only happening for me, not anyone else in all of the economy seat area of the plane!

People around me were acting normally, but when the flight attendant brought me another snack—a hot chocolate chip cookie and a drink—near the end of the flight, well, that was the last straw for many of the people around me. One lady said, "All right, who are you?"

See, I enjoyed the privileges of a first class seat even while I was in coach! Everyone else was surviving on peanuts, but I had a full course dinner WHILE I WAS IN COACH. It's the same in the earth realm. Everyone else may be surviving on peanuts, but you can live above peanuts and have everything you need.

Now, you might be thinking, "The buffet and the airplane story are both great illustrations, Gary, but I'm not satisfied. I don't have everything I need. I *don't* have *all* things." Well then, I'm glad you're reading this book!

Know this: Drenda and I lived in great lack for many years ourselves before we learned the power of a promise.

We lived hand-to-mouth, just barely making it for the first nine years of our marriage. We barely had *anything*, let alone *everything* we needed for those nine *very long* years. We knew about the Kingdom of God. We were Christians, loved God, and went to church. We wanted to experience God's promises in our lives just like anyone else. We just didn't know how. We had to learn that our escape from the earth-curse system was through participating in the divine nature through the power of God's promises.

One of my favorite examples of how the Kingdom operates was years ago when we wanted to purchase a 15-passenger van. We've always had vans, but there was a time when we really desired a 15-passenger van because our kids were getting bigger and they needed some legroom. My family likes to travel, and we like to drive long distances. With all of the camping gear we carry around the country for a family of seven, we really needed the extra space.

The van we had at the time had more than 200,000 miles on it, and we had a camping trip coming up the next year, so we felt it was time to sow and believe for our new van. We came into agreement as a family and prayed for the new van. We also prayed and believed God for the $20,000 it would take to buy it because we wanted to pay cash for it. Because I had learned from the Word of God and from my experiences in deer hunting that we needed to be very specific in our request, we asked for a Chevy Express van in red or bronze with 15,000 miles or less on it.

About three months later, one of the companies I worked for paid me an unexpected bonus check in the amount of $22,000. We knew this was the money we had asked God for, so when a friend invited us to attend an auto auction that would include some Chevy Express vans, we took him up on it.

When we got to the auction, we found that they had eight Chevy Express vans that would be sold that day. Five of those eight matched our color requests—four were red and one was bronze. Only one red van had 15,000 or fewer miles on it, though. When we looked over the van, we found its interior was in perfect condition, but it had a moderate-sized dent in the passenger front door. Drenda was concerned about the dent, so we decided to pass that one up and bid on the bronze van, which had 26,000 miles on it.

The red van with 15,000 miles on it was the first van to go through and, strangely, it didn't sell. But the other three red ones all sold to the same bidder. I found it odd that the first one didn't sell since it only had the small dent and the best mileage of all of the vans. In fact, all of the other red vans had dents in them as well.

As the day went on, the other four vans came through; there were three white ones and the one bronze one we wanted to bid on. Just as the bronze one came through, and we were prepared to jump into the bidding, the auctioneer yelled, "Sold!" and pointed to another gentleman in the room. We were shocked! When we asked the auctioneer what happened, he claimed he didn't see our hands raised to bid. We were standing directly in front of the auctioneer and only seven feet away!

There were no vans left, and we were disappointed. The auctioneer, seeing our disappointment and feeling somewhat responsible for missing our bid for the bronze van, agreed to run the first red van through again if we were interested. I assured Drenda that the dent could easily be fixed, and we agreed to stay and bid. When they brought the red van back through, we were the only bidders. We got our van for the lowest price of them all!

As we reviewed the day's events, there were questions swirling around in my head. Why didn't the red van sell on the first pass? How had the auctioneer completely missed our bid for the bronze van? How did we manage to get the lowest price? Then the Holy Spirit spoke to me. He told me there was only one van there that matched our specific seed: a red Chevy Express van with 15,000 or less miles on it. And it was exactly the one we got!

I realized that the red van didn't sell the first time through the bidding process because it was OUR van, held for us by spiritual law! Although we tried to act in our own human nature and reasoning to get a different van, we had already participated in the divine nature by sowing and praying in agreement for our specific van. I was surprised yet again at how specific the Kingdom operates.

Second Corinthians 1:17-20 says:

> *Do I make my plans in a worldly manner so that in the same breath I say both "Yes, yes" and "No, no"?*

> *But as surely as God is faithful, our message to you is not "Yes" and "No." For the Son of God, Jesus*

Christ, who was preached among you by us—by me and Silas and Timothy—was not "Yes" and "No," but in him it has always been "Yes."

For no matter how many promises God has made, they are "Yes" in Christ. And so through him the "Amen" is spoken by us to the glory of God.

Do you see that? Paul says, "No matter how many promises God has made, they are "Yes" in Christ.

You can't ask too much of God or exhaust His ability!

God wants you to have all of His promises. He wants you to have everything you need for life and godliness. No matter how many promises there are, God made them for you.

So, you don't have to beg! God is faithful and His will has always been "yes" to you as a believer. In Matthew 6:7-8, Jesus said, "Stop babbling like unbelievers, thinking you'll be heard because of your many words. God already knows what you need."

Philippians 4:6 says,

Do not be anxious about anything, but in every situation, by prayer and petition, with thanksgiving, present your requests to God.

Don't beg. Pray with thanksgiving because you know that no matter how many promises God has made—how many things He's already come through on—the answer is still "yes"!

WHAT YOU HAVE TO DO

Chapter 6

So now you know that God's divine power has given you everything you need for life. That's awesome, right? But most people believe God has only given them everything they need as long as they can prove they need it, and that they only need enough to get by. This is wrong!

God has given you everything you need for life through His precious promises. You don't have to prove anything, and God gives you more than enough!

You just have to make the decision that you're going to have what the Bible says. No matter how much failure you have in your past or where you come from, and even if you don't know how to get it, you can determine that you're going to find out how God's Kingdom operates and have everything God says is yours.

God has given you all things to live the life that He's created you to live. The Bible says God's divine power has given you everything you need to live life and to live it with godliness—with righteousness, or as He designed it to be lived. Through the promises, you can participate in the divine nature and escape the corruption of the earth. That means that your family should be whole. That means that your marriage should be whole. That means you should have more than enough money to buy groceries. That means you should have provision. That means you should have purpose. That means you should be at peace.

Remember Abraham? Remember how God told him he would be the father of many nations when he didn't have any children? But Abraham had the promise, and he held onto it. He had the signed check. Galatians 4:21-31 remind us of what happened:

> *Tell me, you who want to be under the law, are you not aware of what the law says? For it is written that Abraham had two sons, one by the slave woman and the other by the free woman. His son by the slave woman was born according to the flesh, but his son by the free woman was born as the result of a divine promise.*
>
> *These things are being taken figuratively: The women represent two covenants. One covenant is from Mount Sinai and bears children who are to be slaves: This is Hagar. Now Hagar stands for Mount Sinai in Arabia and corresponds to the present city of Jerusalem, because she is in slavery with her children. But the Jerusalem that is above is free, and she is our mother. For it is written :*
>
>> *"Be glad, barren woman , you who never bore a child; shout for joy and cry aloud,*

you who were never in labor; because more are the children of the desolate woman than of her who has a husband."

Now you, brothers and sisters, like Isaac, are children of promise. At that time the son born according to the flesh persecuted the son born by the power of the Spirit. It is the same now. But what does Scripture say? "Get rid of the slave woman and her son, for the slave woman's son will never share in the inheritance with the free woman's son." Therefore, brothers and sisters, we are not children of the slave woman, but of the free woman.

We see in verse 23 that Ishmael was born "according to the flesh." Another version says, "in the ordinary way." But look at what it says about Isaac. It says Isaac was born "as the result of a divine promise."

Sarah was advanced in years. In fact, the Bible says she was *beyond* childbearing years. That means that there was nothing happening in her body that could produce a child. It just wasn't possible without God's help, in the same way that it just wasn't possible for Drenda and me to have experienced so many successes. We just aren't that smart on our own!

Without the promises of God, it wouldn't be possible

for Drenda and me to have what we have in the natural. I graduated high school near the very bottom of my class. I hated to study. I had no skills and no talents. I grew up learning the pizza business from my family, but I didn't want to duplicate that. I got an Old Testament degree. That's not very marketable, you know. I didn't have any specialized training. So, how was it possible that we built our home, changed our life, and you're reading this book? How was it possible that Sarah had a baby?

The Scripture tells us: Isaac was conceived by a promise, and he was birthed by the power of God's Spirit. He was born as a result of a promise, and—this is critically important—**a promise from God carries within it the germination ability to produce what it says, regardless of you.**

You may have no ability in yourself to prosper, or to be healed, or whatever the promise says. It may appear hopeless. You may be "beyond childbearing years." The doctors may have said you're going to die. You may have no hope financially. But none of that matters. *It doesn't matter!* Whatever promise you're holding onto may seem absolutely, absolutely, absolutely impossible. You may have tried over and over and over again in your own strength, and fallen flat on your face every single time.

But it doesn't matter. Because there is a way to live above the earth-curse restrictions of time and space. There is a way to live and tap into something that's bigger than life—the Kingdom of God and His promises.

Isaac was in Sarah's womb as the result of a promise, not as the result of anything that she did in her own strength. She didn't change her diet or take special herbs or anything else. She took God's promise, believed it, and she received it. It will work exactly the same way for you. When you take the seed of a promise and put it into your spirit—knowing who God is, that He is good, that He can't lie, and that He wants good for you—and you trust who He is, all by itself the seed of the promise WILL produce what the seed said, but ONLY if you *participate* in that promise, calling things that are not as if they were because God says you have it! Because you have that signed check!

You may have no clue how it's going to happen. Sarah knew it was impossible for her to conceive, but she didn't have to figure it out. She just had to know that God would make it possible. After all, it was His promise and

His glory and goodness that assured her that He had the power and intent to bring it to pass. She just had to put her confidence in Him. The same went for Abraham. He may have known that his wife's womb was as good as dead as far as conceiving was concerned, but he only needed to be convinced that God had the power to do what He said. Abraham and Sarah stood on the promise.

Just like Abraham and Sarah, or Drenda and me, you can see the incredible and enjoy the impossible being birthed in your own life as you believe God's Word and His promises. If you're convinced He has the power to do what He said, regardless of whether or not you know how He's going to do it, and you trust Him to do what He said, and you hold onto the promise, believe the promise, protect the promise, and speak the promise (acting as if you already have what God said He gave you), it will be conceived and birthed into your life.

Once the promise has been conceived, there's a period of time called gestation. During gestation in the natural, we don't know how the baby is forming. A woman may know she's pregnant, but she can't see the baby until it's been birthed. In the same way, we continue to stand on the promise even though we may have no clue how it's forming.

Soon, a mother in the natural will begin to feel the flutter of movement and then the full-on kicks and rolls of the baby, who is growing and preparing for birth. Things may get uncomfortable for the mother. Her body shifts and grows as the baby grows inside her. The growth of the promise is no different. Things may begin to shift. You may get pretty uncomfortable. As you hold to the promise, the Word of God may begin to change your thoughts, realign your priorities, and have you thinking thoughts that are much bigger than yourself. It can be both exciting and scary at the same time.

Then, when it's time—when the baby is ready for birth—he or she is birthed into the natural realm. This whole process is powered and produced by the Spirit of God. Remember, Isaac was conceived as a result of the promise but was born by the power of the Spirit. Just like a mother must continue to nurture the baby in her womb, you must continue to incubate the promise. You must do this until, suddenly, the picture is clear, and you begin to see how the promise has been formed and all of the details. Then, the power of God moves in the situation, He brings the details, reveals the plan, and brings the baby into reality.

But your responsibility doesn't end there.

After you've conceived, and incubated, and birthed the promise by the power of the Spirit, you have to raise it unto the glory of God.

When Drenda and I were broke, we began to believe what God said. Regardless of our past failures, if God said it, we would believe it. We made a decision that we would believe what the Kingdom said about us and not what our circumstances said. We began to apply ourselves to understanding, and we received the promise; and on the inside of me, things began to change.

I had a dream from the Holy Spirit about starting a business I didn't know how to run, but I saw it clearly in my spirit, so I began to incubate it. I started researching it. The idea that was rolling around on the inside of me kept growing bigger and bigger, and the pieces of the puzzle—the form—began to take shape, and we launched the business.

But the birth is never the end of the promise.

God sees the promise as it will be when it's finished, or matured, but we have work to do to get it there. God knew—as we launched the business, and as it matured and we struggled to learn how to operate the business— eventually, it would be the answer to our problem, and it would supply all of the finances that we needed to carry out what we were to do. But the birth is always just one part of the process. We still had a lot to learn. Like parents have to raise a baby, we had to raise the business.

So, we did. We launched it, and we grew it. It was frustrating. We had to learn a lot. Did I say it was frustrating? Because it was! We had never raised an Isaac before. We had to tell ourselves often, "God *said*. He said this was the answer. God *said*." We had to hold on to the promise because there were plenty of times, when we waded out in that deep water, that everything in us was like, "This is scary!" But when the checks started coming in, we saw the promise as it was maturing, and it worked out well.

We looked at 2 Corinthians 1 earlier in Chapter 5, but let's look at verse 20 again:

For no matter how many promises God has made, they are "yes" in Christ. And so through Him the "Amen" is spoken by us to the glory of God.

It says we speak the "Amen" to the glory of God. We say "Amen" to the promise and, as the promise grows up, people see it. People see that you have the answer. The promise manifests itself, and it brings glory to God. It brings the Good News. It brings evidence of God. He gets the credit, and people see it.

Isaiah 61 says God says you are the planting of the Lord, an "oak of righteousness for the display of His splendor." He gave you the promises because the answer to any of your problems is a promise. And He wants people to see evidence of the answers in your life. He wants people to see His glory and His Kingdom, not your problems. That means you've got to live at a higher level than your own kingdom and start enjoying His Kingdom so that, when people see you, they'll scratch their heads and ask, "How did you do that?"

And you can respond and say, "Well, let me tell you about the promises of God. Let me tell you how good He is. Let me tell you how this business got here/how

I was healed/how we got this house/how we paid off our debt. Let me tell you all about it! It's an awesome story!"

IT'S ALREADY FINISHED: HOW YOU CAN SEE RESULTS

Chapter 7

His divine power has given us everything we need for life and godliness through our knowledge of him who called us by his own glory and goodness. Through these he has given us his very great and precious promises, so that through them you may participate in the divine nature and escape the corruption in the world caused by evil desires.

— 2 Peter 1:3-4 (NIV, 1984)

I want to give you an example of the principles we've learned in the last few chapters. What you are about to read is one of the most powerful examples of the power of a promise that I have ever seen in my own ministry. I can't overemphasize how powerful this encounter was and how much it impacted my life, because it concerned my own daughter, Amy. Here, she tells her story:

AMY'S STORY

I've always known that God still heals. In fact, I experienced healing in the past. When I was 8, my family was in a car accident, leaving scars around my eye area. When I started wearing makeup, the scars really bothered me. So I simply said, "God, I don't like these scars, and I'd appreciate it if you'd remove them. Thank you." Literally, I woke up the next morning, and the very noticeable scars had COMPLETELY disappeared. That happened at age 15.

I was about 20 when I felt something changing in my body. Something was wrong, but I didn't know what. My abdomen muscles started becoming hard, protruding more and more. My "innie" belly button became an "outie."

You know how when someone is about to take your picture, you suck in your tummy, pose, and say "cheese"? Well, I stopped being able to pull in my tummy. At all. The muscles in that area of my body became more and more immovable. I thought I must have been gaining weight, so I started eating really healthily, trying to correct the problem. I dropped a few pounds, but the problem got worse.

When I jogged, the muscles all the way down my abs, legs, and back would hurt and become so tight, it was difficult to even stretch. Certain stretches, like pulling my leg up behind me, became almost impossible. Working out with our trainer, we did a lot of ab exercises, and he noticed the problem, but he couldn't figure out why those muscles were not responding. **My abdomen was as hard as a rock.**

I was very self-conscious about my stomach and started dressing to disguise the issue. I started wearing loose-fitting shirts and lots of scarves and jackets. I wouldn't be caught in a tight tee or most swimsuits if I could avoid it.

A year or two into this, my mom took me to an endocrinologist to ask what was up. After feeling my structure and abs, the doctor simply said, "Have your hormones checked, but I just think it's the way you are shaped. Some of us just have a tummy to deal with." In other words, she meant, "Live with it." And that's what I did. I **accepted** the fact that this was just the way I was shaped.

I had my blood tested a few times, and everything always checked out fine. Many possible causes were ruled out, and once again I was just told to live with it. I tried so many things—physical therapy, therapeutic massage, meeting with a kinesiologist/personal trainer—and nothing worked. Although stretching seemed to help my muscles temporarily, it just seemed that my stomach got worse. I stopped my three-mile-per-day jogging routine almost altogether because of the tightness. Plus, I felt embarrassed to jog, except at night, because I didn't want anyone to see the way my stomach looked when exercising.

During this time, I was traveling much more, doing ministry trips both at home and abroad. I also wrote and recorded my first album, and I started doing concerts around Ohio. **Everywhere I went it was inevitable that someone would ask if I was pregnant.** People sometimes got malicious or aggressive in their accusations toward me. One lady became insistent, almost belligerent when I denied being pregnant. The embarrassment I felt every time someone asked that question was very deep. I eventually prepared a standard answer and braced myself for this occurrence during each trip or concert, but I never got used to it. The heart-wrenching thing was that my message was all about purity and abstinence. I was a single woman, for heaven's sake! I stopped doing many concerts because I just didn't want to face this again. Satan was after the two things God had called me to when I was very young: purity and healing ministry.

In 2008, I met the love of my life, and we were married in September, 2009. Jason is the sweetest, kindest, most encouraging guy I have ever met, and his love overcame a lot of the personal hurt I had experienced. He accepted and loved me for who I was, and he never said anything to make me feel there was something "wrong" with my body. But still, the problem seemed to get worse. I became more self-conscious.

After our honeymoon, I started experiencing digestion issues on a daily basis, battling nausea and pain in my abdomen. Finally, Jason made me march back to the doctor. She recommended medication to deal with the symptoms. Something had to change, but I still didn't know what the issue truly was. I didn't take the medications and instead worked on eating a totally non-acidic diet, which helped. **But I didn't want to just cope.**

I attended a healing conference in Texas around early March, 2010, and I decided before I went that I was going to receive my healing for the digestion and nausea issues. After sitting through three days of services, I came to my point of faith, and my sister-in-law prayed for me. From that day on, the nausea stopped completely! I started being able to eat without fear.

This symptom was gone, but my stomach was still hard and round .

My healing had begun, but something in my mind still had to change.

In May, I suffered a severe kidney infection. I found myself hospitalized for a day. Satan was fighting hard for my mind and peace. I knew whatever was causing issues with my abdomen was also putting pressure on my organs in that area. Though I was very sick for ten days, I was determined not to let this stop me from ministering at a conference we were traveling to that weekend in Florida. That first night, I stepped onto the stage feeling very weak, but as the worship started, strength flooded my body.

A few months later, I suffered another infection. That's when I got mad.

I realized that, years ago, I had simply accepted what that first doctor told me, that this was just the way I was. Something was wrong with my body, and I had accepted what Satan had brought against me as the truth, MY truth. The picture of who I WAS had to change.

A chiropractor friend could see something was wrong, and he kindly offered to check out my back and do some x-rays. He showed me where I had indeed lost curvature in my lower back, and where some of the lower vertebrae seemed pushed out of place. Also, one side of my pelvis appeared pushed down and off balance, causing the one leg to be a half-inch shorter than the other.

It looked like something in there was pushing out on all of my bones from the inside. When I saw that x-ray, I finally could see the internal physical effects on my body from whatever this was. I had something to target my faith toward.

When I prayed that night, I heard the word "cyst" roll around in my mind. One of my family members had just had a ten-pound cyst removed, and

I pondered whether this could be the cause of my problems. Surprisingly, no doctor had ever ordered a scan or ultrasound, though we'd brought it up. At this point, it didn't matter, because I was ready to believe God to take care of this problem, whatever it was, without any surgery.

At Faith Life Church, Pastor Gary, (my dad) started teaching a series on healing, called *Live Whole*. Through those weeks of hearing three services every weekend of healing teaching straight from Scripture, I started getting excited. I realized Satan had tricked me into accepting something he had brought against me as "normal." I had allowed him to occupy a piece of my territory. My body was God's temple! It was time to kick this thing out. I was tired of just coping with this problem and its symptoms. I was tired of the embarrassment. I was tired of the emotional pain. Enough was enough.

During that series of healing teaching, I heard my friend Amy Taylor give her testimony about being healed from debilitating daily migraine headaches. She stood on the Scripture Romans 8:11 (KJV), *"But if the Spirit of him that raised up Jesus from the dead dwell in you, he that raised up Christ from the dead shall also quicken your mortal bodies by his Spirit that dwelleth in you."* She said the word "quicken" meant to "restore to its original state." I grabbed hold of that. I wanted my REAL body back!

I decided I would start bombarding my mind with God's Word until I came to the point I had faith and could go down to receive prayer, as James 4 says to do. I had been bombarded by the image of my protruding stomach every day as I dressed myself in things that would hide it. Now I had to see myself healed and normal. I stood on the Scripture that says, *"Do you not know that your bodies are temples of the Holy Spirit, who is in you, whom you have received from God? You are not your own; you were bought at a price. Therefore honor God with your bodies"* (1 Corinthians 6:19-20). Also, *"how God anointed Jesus of Nazareth with the Holy Spirit and power, and how he went around doing good and healing all who were under the power of the devil, because God was with him"* (Acts. 10:38). Everyday during those few weeks, I constantly meditated on healing Scriptures, the promises of God. I knew this problem wasn't God's will. It's all in the Bible! John 10:10 says, *"The thief comes only to steal and kill and destroy; I have come that they may have life, and have it to the full."* My full life was being hindered, and it wasn't God's will.

One Sunday, I went down for prayer, knowing that it was my day to receive my healing. God's power hit me so strongly, I began to weep and shake. Even though when I left that day, the symptoms were still there, I had a new picture of myself. I KNEW I was healed that moment. It was finished. God's Word was MY TRUTH, despite what the facts said externally.

On Tuesday, September 28, I woke up and sat up in bed. My abs felt like I had worked out the day before, but they weren't tight at all. I lay back down and said to Jason, "What did I do yesterday that my muscles are sore?" Jason looked over at me, and a look of shock spread across his sleepy face.

He said, "Amy, look at your stomach! It's...it's flat!"

I looked down and started poking my stomach. For the first time in SIX years, my stomach was flat and SOFT. The muscles that had protruded for so long were back to their normal place! My belly button, which had been pushed out for so long, was an "innie" once again!

OVERNIGHT, I LOST 13 POUNDS AND 9 INCHES FROM MY WAIST! THE CURVE OF MY SPINE INSTANTLY CAME BACK!

The vertebrae weren't sticking out. There was no extra fluid of any kind to show for those missing 13 pounds. I had slept like a baby that night... God just simply removed that thing. If it was a cyst or a tumor or a muscle problem, it was gone. I have before and after pictures to prove it!

I called my mom, and she rushed over. When she walked in to see me standing there, with a waistline that looked totally proportionate to my thin arms and legs, she started crying. So did my family when they saw me that day. So did many friends and church members.

I had new x-rays done of my spine and abdomen. It is clear now from previous x-rays that my organs had been displaced by the growth in my abdomen. My intestines were way up in my rib cage, thus causing digestion issues. Now you can see in the x-rays that all my organs are back where they should be, the curve in my spine is back to normal, and my legs are even. Where there once was a cloudy area in my abdomen, there are normal, clear pictures of my organs.

I AM TOTALLY HEALED!

This was not something that could just *happen*. It wasn't a coincidence. The visible difference overnight was a miracle! It was the LIVING GOD at work. If you have something wrong in your body that you have just accepted as your normal, as your truth, let me encourage you to start reading about the truth in the Bible, about the promises of God. Healing is a promise, and GOD IS A HEALING GOD. He does not change. He is the same yesterday, today, and forever (Hebrews 13:8).

The problem is our own mind, our own doubt, gets in the way. We believe a lie, something a doctor or family member has said, more than we believe what God said. We've grown up hearing about death all our lives. How many medical commercials do you hear on the radio and TV every single day? Turn it off! Shut off the voice of fear! You must bombard that picture of fear, pain, and sickness with the promise of God and the right picture of health. Isaiah 53:5 (NIV, 1984) says, *"But he was pierced for our transgressions, he was crushed for our iniquities; the punishment that brought us peace was upon him, and by his wounds we are healed."*

Not only did I need healed of the physical pain and problem, I needed healed of the emotional pain I had incurred over the years of dealing with this. I had some people to forgive and a bad self-image to let go of. I had to see myself as a whole person before I could ever believe God for healing. I took communion to remind myself of the sacrifice and pain Jesus went through on the cross to bring me healing. Healing isn't just about the physical; it's about the emotional and spiritual. In fact, many times emotional disorders and stress can be the roots of physical problems.

I feel like the woman in the Bible with the issue of blood who went from doctor to doctor, but they couldn't figure out what was wrong with her. She spent all she had on trying to get a cure. (Jason and I have spent thousands since getting married, dealing with symptoms from this stupid thing. But Satan has to return what he stole!) When this sick woman came to Jesus and reached for Him in faith, all that changed. *"Jesus turned and saw her. ' Take heart, daughter,' he said, 'your faith has healed you.' And the woman was healed from that moment"* (Matthew 9:22, NIV, 1984).

God is so amazing, and I will live all my days loving Him. He is my hero. And I will never stop telling this story. And no one can ever convince me that God isn't real, because I've seen with my own eyes His work, and **no one can ever tell me that His promises aren't true, or that He doesn't heal, because He healed me.**

Amy's story is amazing, and these photographs only confirm it. The photo on the left shows what Amy looked like when she went to bed on Monday, September 27. The photo on the right was taken Tuesday, September 28 after she woke up healed. I get to see the evidence of her healing in person! It's AMAZING!

Now, there's a part of Amy's story I really want you to plainly see—when she was prayed for, *nothing* changed. In fact, nothing changed for almost TWO WEEKS! But Amy, being convinced of God's ability and intent, took His promise as a finished work and, once prayed for, began to act and speak as if she was already healed. She had the signed check in her pocket, and she was sure it was good.

Again, compare this to how most people talk about the promises of God. They say, "I'm believing that God *will* heal me," or "He *is* healing me," or "I know that He *will* heal me," but that's all in the future tense. This is where people miss it! We need to receive the promises based on God's glory and goodness as good. Instead of waiting for God to do something, we need to realize that He already has, and it is finished!

We simply need to *participate* in the divine nature, calling things that are not as though they were in order to release heaven into the earth realm. Remember, simply confessing what God says isn't enough. The formula by itself won't get the job done anymore than just having the right wires in the walls of your house will power your washing machine. Those wires have to be connected to the right power source in order to bring the right results.

Being fully persuaded in your heart is what brings heaven's jurisdiction to earth. When you speak with heaven's authority, you'll see heaven on earth.

Drenda and I started *Faith Life Now*, our television broadcast, to tell people the Good News of the Kingdom of God. Today, Faith Life Now reaches every time zone in the world every day of the week with the exciting Good News. Our own excitement will never run out, especially because we're still seeing the Kingdom impact lives all around the world!

It's our hope that this book will significantly impact your life, because you have these "very great and precious promises" from the One who has all power, all authority, and cannot lie! His name is Jesus!

You can find more life-changing resources about the Kingdom at garykeesee.com. While you're there, contact me and let me know how this book impacted your life. I'd love to hear from you!

Gary Keesee

ABOUT THE AUTHOR

Gary Keesee is a television host, author, international speaker, financial expert, successful entrepreneur, and pastor who has made it his mission to help people win in life, especially in the areas of faith, family, and finances.

After years of living in poverty, Gary and his wife, Drenda, discovered the principles of the Kingdom of God, and their lives were drastically changed. Together, under the direction of the Holy Spirit, they created several successful businesses and paid off all of their debt. Now, they spend their time declaring the Good News of the Kingdom of God around the world through Faith Life Now, their organization that exists to motivate, educate, and inspire people from all walks of life and backgrounds to pursue success, walk out their God-designed purposes, and leave positive spiritual and moral legacies for their families.

Faith Life Now produces two television programs—*Fixing the Money Thing* and *Drenda*—as well as practical resources, conferences, and speaking events around the world.

Gary is also the president and founder of Forward Financial Group and the founding pastor of Faith Life Church, which has campuses in New Albany and Powell, Ohio.

Gary and Drenda, their five adult children and their spouses, and their grandchildren all reside in Central Ohio.

For additional resources by both Gary and Drenda, visit FaithLifeNow.com.

FINANCIAL REVOLUTION CONFERENCES

If you're a pastor or leader in your church, you probably have plenty of vision for your ministry. But do you have the money or resources you need to support the vision?

If your church is like most churches, the answer is probably *not quite* or even *no*.

Why?

We've found one of the biggest reasons is DEBT. So many Christians are being held *hostage* by debt.

Your people *WANT* to financially support the ministry and vision of your church, but many of them are living paycheck to paycheck with no hope of breaking free.

We can help.

For more than 25 years now, we've been working with churches of all sizes, helping them reach their goals and see their visions for their ministries become reality. And the best part is that this is completely free!

We help churches by helping their people. We can help *your church* by helping *your people*.

Learn more at **ftmtevent.com**.

Gary Keesee went from being completely desperate financially and physically to healthy and whole, paying cash for cars, building his home free from debt, starting multiple companies, and teaching hundreds of thousands of people about Kingdom living each week through television, ministry, and books just like this one.

What changed for Gary and how can it change YOUR LIFE?

Your answers are in the pages of THIS book series.

This isn't just another set of books with tips on how to fix your finances.

Full of fresh revelation, powerful examples from the Word of God, and inspiring personal stories about Gary and others who applied the foundational teachings from these five Kingdom principles in their own lives and experienced drastic change as a result, this series of books was written to help YOU experience real change in EVERY area of your life.

No matter your situation, there are answers. It's never too late.

You can have your own amazing story!

Join Gary Keesee on this incredible five-part journey of discovery that will completely revolutionize YOUR life… just like it did his.

This set contains paperback versions of Gary's complete *Your Financial Revolution* book series:

- *Your Financial Revolution: The Power of Allegiance*

- *Your Financial Revolution: The Power of Rest*

- *Your Financial Revolution: The Power of Strategy*

- *Your Financial Revolution: The Power of Provision*

- *Your Financial Revolution: The Power of Generosity*

Get your copy of the complete *Your Financial Revolution* five-book series at GaryKeesee.com.

Printed in Great Britain
by Amazon

37156021R00056